BEHIND THE SMILE

How Pain Prepared Me For My Purpose

May God continue to keep and bless you!

With Lots of Love,
Lisa ♡

LisaCarterSpeaks.Com

LISA HENDERSON-CARTER

For details email joan@victoriousyoupress.com

or visit us at www.victoriousyoupress.com

DEDICATION:

Son, my first book is dedicated to you. There were moments I struggled to write about, but I embraced every part because it made me who I am today. You didn't ask to be brought into this world, and I wasn't prepared to give you everything you needed, however, we made it through some tough times. You were five years old when I graduated from high school. There were times when life got the best of me, and I didn't think I had the strength to carry on, but you were depending on me. Not only were you depending on me, you watched every move I made. Thank you for keeping me on my toes. Because of you, I had even more of a reason to pursue my purpose. No matter what life throws your way, always remember, greatness is flowing through your veins. You, too, were born for a purpose. I love you, son.

ACKNOWLEDGEMENTS

I thank God for:

- Keeping and protecting me during some of the most challenging times of my life

- My mother instilling the importance of respecting adults and keeping my education a priority

- My family and friends who encouraged, loved me without judgment, and helped pick up the broken pieces

- Every person who provided a place for my son and me to live

- Every medical/mental health professional, social worker, case manager, mentor, who provided exceptional care and a genuine concern for me and my son's well-being, including but not limited to the Department of Social Services, Boston's Children's Services, Boston Medical Center (formerly Boston City Hospital) Pediatric Department, Teen & Tot Program, and Big Brother/Big Sister of America

- The exposure to opportunities that supported my growth and development through the following programs/organizations: Cooper Community Center, Boys & Girls Club,

ProTech Boston, ABCD, Adolescent Pregnancy Prevention Intervention Network

- The English High School staff for supporting me through my journey and offering an amazing program designed to help young parents succeed against the odds

- My husband and children for reminding me why I needed to write my story

INTRODUCTION:

My mother always said, "Nothing goes between your legs but a washcloth and some soap!" I didn't understand the significance of her statement until I got the results of my pregnancy test. Getting that news was gut-wrenching. I had just celebrated my thirteenth birthday, and this was NOT a gift I felt good about! The thought of possibly being a mother scared me. I couldn't imagine what having a baby at such a young age would be like, let alone feel like! So many thoughts rushed through my head as the pit of my stomach grew more and more unsettled, thinking about the reality of a baby growing inside of my fragile body. I felt numb, alone, and confused. My mind started racing, my heart pumped twice as fast, but my body was completely still. I felt like I was in a bad dream, a dream I wished I could wake up from, but I wasn't dreaming. I was fully awake, completely at a loss for words and had no idea what to do next. Although I was in disbelief when I received the news, I had a feeling I was pregnant; after all, we didn't use any birth control. This was real. This was my reality. This was my responsibility. Within seconds, my life had taken on a whole new meaning, and I asked myself, "How did I end up here?"

TABLE OF CONTENTS

PART 1

I AM INNOCENT

LISA HENDERSON-CARTER

Earliest Memories

My name is Lisa Latrice Henderson-Carter. I was born on August 13th, 1975, at Boston City Hospital in Boston, Massachusetts. My birth certificate only has my mother's name on it. I assume my father's name isn't listed because they weren't on good terms when I was born. I could only imagine how I looked as a baby because I didn't have any baby pictures growing up, but my mother said I had chubby cheeks, dimples, and a head full of hair.

I was a sickly baby and suffered from bronchitis, which later turned into asthma. My mother spent countless hours with me at the hospital because of my respiratory illness, but she said that didn't stop me from hollering at the top of my lungs when I wanted something!

When I was three years old, my mother, older brother, and I lived in Orchard Park Projects (O.P.), one of Boston's public housing communities within walking distance from Boston City Hospital. O.P. was made up of three-story brick buildings that were so close together you could walk through one building to get to the other. I distinctly remember walking up the gloomy, dark, urine scented halls with my mother to our apartment. Sometimes someone mopped the halls with bleach or Pine Sol, which temporarily killed the odor. Each building had front and back entrances that led outside to the inner courtyard. There were rows of clotheslines where residents hung their laundry out to dry and a few concrete benches to sit on. Even though we didn't have a playground, kids always found something to do.

One day while playing outside, we came across a man lying beside the dumpster. We watched him for a while because he was completely still. The next thing you know, everyone took off running as fast as they could because we were afraid. The image of seeing him just lying there never left my memory. Growing up, I always referred to him as the "dead man." As an adult, I often wondered if he could have been drunk or homeless and just needed a place to sleep.

Around the same time, I also fell into a bathtub of running water while watching it fill up. I don't remember my mother being around, but her friend, James, came in and pulled me out as I choked and gasped for air. He patted me on my back repeatedly until I stopped coughing. It's a good thing he was close enough to hear the commotion coming from the bathroom!

My brother and I attended Cooper Community Center, an early childhood development program. Cooper Center opened up my world to the love of learning. I absolutely LOVED going to school. I remember playing with other children, coloring, reading books, and just enjoyed being a child. Most times, my mother walked us to school, but sometimes we walked to Dudley Station, which was the next block over, to take the bus. The ride was only about three stops away, but it felt like an adventure as I sat on my mother's lap, looking out the window. When we arrived, my mother signed us in, then left. I don't remember her coming to my classroom or spending much time there.

Moving with Da-Da

When I was about five, we moved a couple of miles away to Humboldt Avenue with my grandfather, who we called Da-Da. Da-Da's leg had been amputated and my mother moved in to help take care of him.

Da-Da lived in a small studio apartment on the first floor. The space was just big enough for him to get around in his wheelchair. I don't even remember where we slept while we lived with him, probably in the small living room space, which was connected to the kitchen. I loved Da-Da. He always made me feel special. Whenever he'd see me, he'd say, "Hey, Lee-Lee, come give me a kiss," and I'd run over and give him a kiss on the cheek. Sometimes he gave me a few quarters to buy something from the corner store, which really put a smile on my face!

Shortly after moving in with Da-Da, someone contacted social services and filed a 51-A report for abuse and negligence against my mother. I'm not sure what happened that led to the report, but they were concerned about me and my brother's well-being. Our case was assigned to a social worker named Judy, who was an older Jewish woman with short curly hair. Judy helped my mother quickly get her own apartment in the same building on the third floor.

Our apartment was a small, one-bedroom with a kitchen just big enough for the stove, refrigerator, and a small washing machine. My mother made the best of the small space, though. She turned the living room into a multi-purpose room where her full-size mattress and box spring sat on the floor, a small round wooden table was in the corner with a twelve-inch black and white TV on it and the sofa against the wall. My brother and I shared the bedroom, which barely fit two twin-sized beds. There were two windows and a small closet in our room. Our apartment was located in the back of the building, so we could hear and see children playing hide-and-seek or dodge ball in the inner courtyard. We even heard families speaking loudly from their windows or back porches and could smell the aroma of fried chicken or bacon if someone was cooking.

Elementary School Days

I can remember my first day of kindergarten as if it were yesterday. I went to David A. Ellis Elementary in Roxbury. The Ellis was one of several schools that kids in the neighborhood attended. We lived within a two-mile radius of the school, so we were in the walker zone. On my first day of kindergarten, my mother walked my brother, who was in the second grade, and me to school. I was so excited about going to my new school but was also nervous. When we arrived, my mother stood near the side entrance on the sidewalk until the teacher filed us into the building. I looked back at her and waved goodbye as she walked away.

My kindergarten teacher's name was Mr. Felante. He was a heavy-set, white man with a full mustache. His classroom was fun and structured. Mr. Felante expected his students to work together, respect one another, and listen to instructions the first time. Being in his class provided me with a safe environment and

I enjoyed going until my new friend, Kenya, said something that hurt my feelings.

Kenya and I always played together until the day I came to school with my hair in about eight single braids or plaits, as my godmother, Stella, called them. That weekend I stayed at Stella's house. She washed and then braided my hair. I didn't have any hairballs, ribbons, or barrettes, just plain braids. I remember looking in the mirror after she was done, and I did not feel pretty.

Later that morning, Kenya confirmed my feelings about my hair. While we were playing in class, she looked at me and said, "I'm not your friend anymore."

I asked, "Why?"

"Because your hair is ugly," she said.

My feelings were hurt. I couldn't understand why my hair would cause her not to be my friend. I couldn't wait to get home to ask my mother to take my hair out, but she was not concerned about what other people thought about my hair. Later in life, I thought about a quote we used to say, "Sticks and stones may break my bones, but names will never hurt me." Well, that was a lie. I was hurt.

Not long after I started kindergarten, my mother let us walk to school by ourselves. She told us to stay together and not to talk to strangers. We walked in a group with other kids who lived in our building. Our walk was fun but sometimes stressful. During that time, there were reports of children in our neighborhood being lured and snatched by people dressed as clowns who drove around in vans; therefore, we were always on the lookout. We also had to keep an eye out for "Freddie the Raper," a man who lived in the neighborhood and dressed in women's clothing to deceive children. Sometimes, while walking to school, we'd start running because someone would say, "Freddie the Raper" was coming! All of the kids were afraid because we had to pass his street in order to get to school. Once we got close to school, we'd run as fast as we could until we arrived. Then, we knew we were safe.

One day we went to play at Franklin Park, our neighborhood park. Kids always ran quickly to be the first ones to get a swing. We were so focused on the swings that we didn't notice "Freddie" sitting on the bench. After playing for a while, one of the older kids noticed him watching us. With fear in her eyes, she whispered, "That's "Freddie the Raper! At the count of three, run!" We jumped off those swings so fast and ran like never before! When we looked back, he was standing there watching us through the fence disguised as a woman with a dress, a wig, and a pair of glasses. Those were scary times. All we wanted to do was enjoy being kids, but we had to watch our surroundings carefully.

Latchkey Kids

After school, kids met in front of the school to walk home together. Sometimes, we stopped at the corner store to buy snacks. I usually didn't have any money, but I always hoped someone would offer to share. Most times, no one shared their snacks, and asking for some would get you a very loud, "STOP BEGGING!" remark, which was so embarrassing.

There were times when my mother wasn't home after school, so she gave my brother a key that he wore around his neck on a shoestring. If my mother wasn't there, I'd rush to the refrigerator hoping to find something to eat before starting my homework. Other times, we knew she was home because we heard her singing at the top of her lungs or cussing somebody out for "pissing her off!" That's when we knew she had been drinking. When she drank, she was loud and unpleasant to be around. That's when "Lucy," her nickname, was in full effect! When sober, she was quiet, irritable, and didn't want to be bothered most times. Her personality was like night and day if she had been drinking. Having a drink in her system helped her "feel" better. The problem was she didn't have a limit. Once she had one drink, she had to have more.

Even though my mother drank most of the time, we were expected to attend school every day. When the alarm clock went off, we woke up, got ready, then left the house in time to eat breakfast at school. We moved throughout the house quietly not wanting to wake her up. She usually had been drinking the night before, so we didn't see her until we returned home. After school, we were expected to come straight home, take off our school clothes, then complete our homework. We couldn't even think about asking to go outside to play until our work and house cleaning were done.

When we got our report cards, we were expected to "come through the door with A's & B's. She also expected us to be respectful and respond to adults with a "yes or no," not "huh or yeah."

Corner Store

When I was seven, my mother sent me to the corner store to buy cigarettes. She'd say, "Lee Lee, I need you to go get me a pack of cigarettes and HURRY UP before I have a nicotine fit!" I had no idea what that meant, but I knew it meant I'd better hurry back! She'd give me $1.10 for a box of Newport 100's and sometimes, she'd write a list and give me her food stamps to buy a few things.

I hated going to the store with food stamps because I was too embarrassed to be seen using them. Back then, food stamps came in a booklet. If you were using more than a dollar coupon, the cashier had to witness you physically tear the coupon out of the book. This process was to prevent food stamp fraud but also brought unwanted attention to the buyer. Whenever I went to the store, I'd get the items on the list, then stall until the other shoppers left the store.

There were times, however, when my mother would give me fifty cents or a dollar to buy myself something. Now, that made the trip worth going! My favorite things to buy were a maple walnut ice cream cone with chocolate jimmies, a pickle, sour cream and onion chips, a blue teenie juice, pineapple Now and Later candy, a sour apple blow pop, or a pack of coconut cookies. Of course, I didn't have enough to buy everything, so I had to decide what I wanted most. I typically bought the items that were least expensive, so I could get more bang for my buck.

There was nothing like that walk back home, though. I'd dig in my brown paper bag and start eating my bag of chips or candy while paying close attention as I crossed the streets. After all, I HAD to make it back home with my mother's cigarettes!

Those trips to the corner store showed up at the dental office. There was a neighborhood dentist on the first floor in a duplex apartment building one block from our house. I had several cavities filled there. All of my cavities were filled with the metal filling material used years ago. As I got older, I realized how unsightly having a mouth full of metal fillings was when I laughed, but I am glad I received dental care, or I probably wouldn't have any teeth in my mouth now.

Community

Growing up on Humboldt Avenue was memorable. The building we lived in was conjoined with another identical building. Because we lived on the top floor, there were stairs leading to the roof that were close to our front door. Whenever my mother visited friends who lived in the other building, she'd cross over from the roof. When she went to the other building, I always got nervous thinking about the possibility of her falling off the building or slipping on the gravel and hurting herself because she had been drinking. Miraculously, she always made it back home.

Our apartment building was our community. There were several adults who kept an eye on the children in our building. Ms. Gladys and her husband, Jimbo, were an older couple that lived to the left of us. They were also heavy drinkers, but loved children and had several grandchildren of their own. My mother hung out at their house often and we sometimes ate Sunday dinner there.

Ms. Diane, her husband, and two children lived on the second floor. They were also drinkers and sometimes argued loud enough for the neighbors to hear, but both parents worked, and their home seemed more stable than ours.

Jesse, a man who lived alone on the first floor, didn't say much; he just nodded his head and grinned. Although Jesse seemed strange, he never did or said anything to make me feel uncomfortable. He'd just open his door if he heard commotion or peep out his peep hole.

There were about twenty other kids who lived in our apartment building. If there was inclement weather, we'd play in the building. We jumped double-dutch rope, played hide and seek, or roller-skated up and down the hallway. There were front and back staircases and a dark, creepy basement that made hide and seek even more fun. We knew how to create our own entertainment while yelling and screaming throughout the building. Sometimes if we got too loud and rowdy, parents would make their children go in the house, then the fun would be over.

Weekends were the best, though, especially if the weather was nice. The adults sat outside on the front stoop, listened to old school music, and drank their adult beverages wrapped in a brown paper bag. As kids, we knew if the adults were hanging out, it was going to be a fun night. We'd run up and down the street until it was time to go in. Some nights we played outside as late as 11 p.m.

Another neighbor that looked out for the children was a man named Jimmie who lived to the right of us. He was a clean-cut, church going man who worked and didn't get involved in neighborhood drama. Jimmie introduced us to his church's summer camp program at Grace Community Church. Grace had a van that picked up neighborhood children and took them to camp. I enjoyed going to camp because it gave me something to do. We played outside, participated in activities, and learned bible stories.

On one occasion, while playing outside the church, a dog came out of nowhere and started chasing the kids. Everyone ran except my younger cousin, Kiona, who had just started coming to camp with us. She couldn't keep up with us, so I picked her up and started running as fast as I could before losing my balance and falling. I fell on her, and her back was scratched from the asphalt. She cried hysterically as we walked quickly into the church. I wasn't hurt physically, but I cried because she was hurt, and I felt responsible for dropping her. An adult cleaned her back, put a bandage on it, then sent us to Bible study. During the lesson, Kiona laid her head on my lap and fell asleep as I sat there with a heart full of sadness.

My brother and I started attending church with Jimmie on Sundays as well. Although my mother didn't go, she trusted him to take us. Jimmie served as an usher, and I joined the choir. The

13

choir was called the Junior Ensemble. I distinctly remember an occasion when the choir marched in singing for the church's anniversary. We sang, "We are the Junior Ensemble, and we're glad you're here. This is our anniversary, and we made it through the year. Oh yes, we made it. Oh yes, we did. Thank God, we made it. Oh yes, we did!"

When we FINALLY got to the choir stand, each person got into formation according to height. Since I was one of the youngest members, I ended up being in the front row. We continued clapping and singing, "He brought us, kept us, brought us, kept us!" I was so excited that I kept singing the hook over and over again without realizing we were directed to stop singing. When the choir director finally got my attention, I realized I was the only one still singing my heart out, front and center stage! Everyone smiled, and some laughed hysterically as I looked around with complete embarrassment. Nevertheless, it felt good deep down in my soul.

Spending the Night

Some weekends, I stayed at my godmother, Stella's house, who lived in Franklin Field Projects, a few miles from my house. Although she was a single mom and lived on a fixed income, her home felt and looked different than some of the other homes in the neighborhood. When you walked in the front door, everything was bright and clean. You could smell the freshness and the aroma of clean clothes drying in the air. Her house was very organized.

She had a system where she washed clothes on Saturday, then ironed, and hung them up on Sunday for the upcoming week.

I always got excited when my mother told me to pack a bag for the weekend. There were times when she dropped me off at her house, but most times, Stella sent a taxi to pick me up from my house. The ride was adventurous. I was only eight years old and could barely see the cab driver's head over the barrier, however, I memorized the route and paid close attention as the driver drove down Seaver Street to Blue Hill Avenue, then turned left onto Stratton Street. Once I arrived, I felt relieved knowing I got there safely. I'd get out of the cab, then yell her name as loud as I could until she came to the window to drop down the cab fare from the third-floor.

Stella's only child, Stephanie, was a couple of years younger than me. Having someone close to my age made my visits fun. We didn't have any worries. As kids, all we wanted was twenty-five cents to buy an icee from "The Icee Lady," who lived a few buildings over. We'd walk over to her building, then yell at the top of our lungs, "ICEE LADY!" She'd come to the window, tell us what flavors she had, then let a basket down with a rope attached from the third floor to collect our money. After we dropped our money in the basket, she'd raise it back up, then send down our icees. My favorite flavor was coconut. It was creamy, sweet, and had tiny coconut pieces in it. She also had grape, cherry, and lemonade. After we received our icee, we'd walk back to play outside with the other kids or watch the boys play marbles in the dirt.

After playing outside all day, we'd go home, take a bath and eat dinner. Sometimes we cooked our own food and experimented using some of the kitchen gadgets. There was always food in the house, so we had a variety of options to choose from. After eating, we cleaned up, but most times my godmother cleaned everything. Stephanie didn't have much to do around the house. This sometimes annoyed me. I thought she was spoiled and could not understand why she didn't wash and iron her own clothes or make up her own bed! This didn't look anything like how we did things at my house!

Stella was a smoker and sent us to the corner store to buy cigarettes too, but she always gave us enough money to buy something for ourselves, so I didn't mind. Stephanie, on the other hand, didn't like going as much. She usually huffed and puffed as we walked down Stratton Street. Stella had a few drinks on the weekend but didn't go out much or have a lot of different people in and out of her house. Every now and then, her boyfriend would slip in at night, but other than that, she people watched and talked on the phone for hours with her friend who lived a few buildings down the street.

Most of the kids in the neighborhood also came from single-parent homes. There were usually three or more siblings, and you could tell the struggle was real. They, like myself, didn't always have money to get snacks from the corner store but still managed to make the most out of their situation.

Even though we were in the heart of a gang turf war between Franklin Field and Franklin Hill, another housing project less than a half-mile away, we still ran up and down the street without a care in the world. Every now and then, we'd overhear teenagers talking about someone who got jumped or stabbed. There were sneakers tied together that hung from the powerlines up and down the street. I'd look up and wonder why someone would throw a good pair of sneakers up there! As I got older, I learned the sneakers signified a gang marking their block or represented someone in their crew who died.

Auntie Sheila's

I also loved visiting my Aunt Sheila's house, my mother's younger sister. She lived near Grove Hall on Cheney Street, a few blocks away from my house. Auntie Sheila was upbeat and so much fun to be around. She loved playing music, singing, and had a beautiful voice. When we visited, she'd turn on her strobe light and let us dance "like no one was watching" to songs like Planet Rock and Run DMC. Our favorite dance was called "The Tick." We battled each other and created different dances like "The Birthday Cake," where we mimicked the gestures of making a cake while ticking through the movements. Of course, we pretended to eat it when it was done!

My younger cousin, Kiona, was my aunt's only child. Kiona had so many toys and fun things to play with; including a big wheel we loved riding down the hill. Sometimes while playing outside, other kids from the neighborhood tried to take her toys and she would run in the house to tell my aunt. My aunt was a lot like my mother; she didn't take NO mess! She would tell us, "You better whoop their ass, or I will whoop yours!" We definitely didn't want that, so we learned how to handle it on our own.

I remember the smell of incense and weed burning in the house and always wondered why she and her friends always seemed to be having a really good time when they were together. One day, my aunt left the house for a short time, and I noticed a joint in the kitchen drawer. I immediately showed it to my brother and asked him if he wanted to smoke it.

He said, "No, we will get in trouble."

I said, "She won't know!" I lit it on the kitchen stove, started smoking it, then passed it to him. He decided to try it, then gave it back to me. Shortly after, I heard the front door open. It was my aunt! I ran into the bedroom and placed the lit joint under the bed.

She walked into the kitchen and yelled, "Y'all been smoking my reefer!?" She went right to the kitchen drawer and checked where she left it and noticed it wasn't there. I got the lit joint from under the bed and handed it to her. She called my mother and told her what happened. My mother walked to my aunt's and was there in ten minutes. She was furious! When she found out my brother smoked some, too, she was really upset because he didn't get into too much mischief. I, on the other hand, always managed to almost "get my teeth knocked down my throat!" Shortly after my mother got to my aunt's, the phone rang, and it was my grandfather, Da-Da. He must have gotten the word about what happened and somehow managed to talk her out of whooping us. I'm so glad he did.

Yvonne's

By this time, I was in the third grade and became friends with a girl named Yvonne. Yvonne came to school later in the school year. She was so pretty and always looked put together. We were in the same class and, to my surprise, ended up living on the same street, just one block down. We spent a lot of time together at school, and eventually, I spent weekends at her house. Yvonne's home felt safe and warm. It was clean, and there was always food in the house.

On the weekends, her parents bought take-out for dinner or ordered a sub or cheeseburger and fries from the neighborhood liquor store. Yvonne's parents worked every day. They had structure and expectations in their house. Yvonne was responsible for washing dishes, cleaning the tub after taking a bath, and keeping her room clean. If the Kool-Aid was low, she made more and made it just how she was taught; two packs of mix and two cups of sugar in a gallon sized container. It always came out just right. After spending so much time at Yvonne's, I was no longer considered a guest. I was expected to contribute to household chores as well. If they weren't done, that meant Yvonne couldn't have company, and God knows I didn't want that!

On the weekends, her parents had a few drinks and hung out on their front stoop while we jumped double-dutch, painted our nails, or sang along with the words on the back cover of a record album. Yvonne lived so close to me that I could see my building from her house. When we played outside, I sometimes saw my mother walking down the street on her way to the liquor store. If she was sober, I would feel proud. If she was drunk, that meant she was liable to say or do anything. That was when I would run around the corner to hide until she got down the street.

I really enjoyed staying at Yvonne's house. As time went along, I asked if I could stay during the week since we went to the same school. Whenever her parents said yes, I'd ask Yvonne to come with me to ask my mother. I'd pack a bag as quickly as I could before my mother changed her mind.

I felt safe at Yvonne's. We were expected to take baths, help clean up, and complete our homework. One Christmas, her parents bought us the same outfit, black pants with small hearts on them and a red shirt. I LOVED our matching outfits. We often wore it to school on the same day. Yvonne was a real friend, and I loved spending time with her family so much that I didn't want to go back home.

That year, our class went on a field trip to go apple picking. I had eaten apples before, but the thought of picking my own from a tree was exciting. All of the kids were eager and talked about all the snacks they were going to bring to eat while on the bus. When the teacher gave us the permission slip to be signed by our parents, I wondered if I'd be able to go because there was a $3.00 fee to pick apples. I knew my mother didn't always have extra money and immediately started thinking of ways to ask for help to go. My first plan was to look in the creases of the couch at home where I'd sometimes find change that fell out of someone's pocket.

When I got home, I asked my mother if she could sign my permission slip and told her I had to pay to go. She went into her stash/change jar and counted enough change for me to go. I put the money and my permission slip in an envelope. And with a smile, I gave it to my teacher the next day. I was going apple picking. That experience was one of the best childhood memories I ever had.

r

PART 2

I AM CURIOUS

LISA HENDERSON-CARTER

Just Curious

I heard and saw a lot at an early age. I guess being exposed to drugs and alcohol piqued my curiosity. Smoking marijuana, cigarettes, and snorting raw grits in my attempt to imitate using cocaine, were things I saw those closest to me do. As I choked and gasped from the burning sensation in my nose and throat, I quickly learned that raw grits did not belong up my nostrils. The whole time I was hoping my mother didn't come into my room to ask me what was wrong. Later in life, I had a newfound respect for the term "curiosity killed the cat." My curiosity almost definitely got the best of me.

Womanhood

I started my menstrual cycle when I was in the fifth grade. My teacher, Mrs. Thompson, was a tall African American woman with a jheri curl. She demanded order in her classroom, which was exactly what we needed before moving on to middle school. Mrs. Thompson loved her students, and we knew she cared about us. I witnessed her concern for me when I told her something was wrong after coming back from using the bathroom.

With concern in my eyes, I said, "Mrs. Thompson?"

"Yes," she said.

"When I wiped myself, I saw something."

Without hesitation, she wrote a pass and sent me to the nurse's office. I was so uncomfortable, and although my mother talked with me a little about it, I felt unprepared.

On my walk home from school, I told my friends I started my menstrual cycle. I wasn't the first one to start, so it wasn't news to the other girls. As I got closer to home, fear settled in because I didn't know how my mother was going to respond. I decided to stop at my friend Coryn's house before going home. When I walked in the house, Coryn told her grandmother I started my cycle.

"Honey, when I got mine, I kept wiping and wiping, hoping it would go away, but it kept on coming," her grandmother said. She told me it was a natural part of womanhood and reassured me that everything would be alright.

I pulled myself together and went home. I walked in the house, and my mother was there. She was sober.

"Mummy, guess what?" I said.

"What, you started your period?" she said.

I was relieved that she already knew what was going on with me! I'm not sure who told her, maybe the school nurse? Either way, I was glad she wasn't upset or yelling at me; instead, she sent my brother to the store to buy menstrual products for me. Although my mother talked with me about the "birds and the bees," I didn't quite understand. She told me starting my period meant I could get pregnant. I didn't ask any questions; I just kept it in the back of my mind.

My Mother

My mother's name is Gail. She was a beautiful woman, especially when she was sober and took care of herself. I don't know much about her past because she didn't talk about it. When she was a teenager, she experienced seeing her mother go from a working woman to barely recognizing her after a brain injury caused by a fall. She grew up in a home and community surrounded by alcohol and drug abuse and started drinking at an early age. Her mother, Jimmie Mae, and father, Ralph (Da-Da), were married and had four children. My mother was the second of four siblings.

Growing up, I remember her always saying her father was a white man! I never understood why she said it, but her complexion was definitely much lighter than her siblings, so I always wondered if it was true. When I was an adult, I told Da-Da what my mother always said and asked if it was true. He said my mother did have a different father, but he wasn't a white man. He was a friend of my grandfather.

Grocery Shopping

As a little girl, I remember seeing my mother lying in bed sucking her thumb while watching soap operas, such as General Hospital or One Life to Live. She worked a couple of days a week as a homemaker, but other than that, she hung out with friends and drank Wild Irish Rose, Colt 45, or gin. When she received her monthly welfare benefits, she purchased a money order for rent, dropped it off at the rental office, then went food shopping at Family Foodland in Washington Park Mall or Farmers Market in Mattapan. Sometimes she took me shopping with her. We'd get on the bus, ride to our destination, then move swiftly through the store. While shopping, my mother was focused and knew exactly what she needed to buy. She kept a straight face most of the time, which allowed others to know she was there to handle her business.

After shopping, we took a gypsy cab back home. Gypsies were locals who used their personal cars to make a few extra dollars transporting people around the city. The moment we walked out of the grocery store, there were cars lined up waiting for customers. All the drivers were men, men I didn't know. I never felt comfortable getting into their cars and always hoped we would make it home safely. My mother, on the other hand, never looked concerned at all. She would direct the driver to our house, then give him a few dollars for the ride. Most times, the driver would help unload the groceries before taking off quickly to pick up another customer.

Grocery shopping days were the best. Some of my mother's staple items were pinto beans, neck bones, fried chicken wings, or chicken and rice cooked together in one big pot. I wasn't a fan of the beans and neckbones, but I loved her fried chicken! She used canned Crisco or lard to fry the chicken. After she was done, she poured the used grease back into the can to use again. She didn't cook all the time, but when she did, we appreciated it. Other times, we were on our own to make a bowl of cereal, ramen noodles, or a bologna and cheese sandwich.

Every now and then, the church across the street held a food pantry and gave out peanut butter, a huge block of cheese, rice, cereal, and powdered milk. These items came in standard white and black packaging and were useful. I could not stomach the dry milk, but the cheese! Oh my, the cheese was so good. We made THE BEST grilled cheese sandwiches with that "government cheese," as people called it.

There were times during the month when the food stamps were low, and there was very little or no food in the house. The only thing in the refrigerator was ketchup, mayonnaise, and a jug of cold water filled up by my mother for her hangover or "hotbox," as she called it. Sometimes there were a few dead cockroaches that managed to crawl into the refrigerator. I guess they were looking for food, too! My brother and I made the best of a not-so-good situation. If there were a couple of end slices of bread left, we toasted it in the oven, put some butter on it, then sprinkled a little sugar on top. We also made sugar water if there was nothing to drink. I hated the taste of plain water, so most times, I didn't drink anything. This probably explains why I passed out while waiting to board the bus to overnight camp one summer.

Lisa Lips

My mother often called me Lisa Lips, "Because you talk too damn much!" she would say. I had an opinion about most things and would sometimes say things or make gestures that led to a pop in the mouth. Sometimes, I got out of line and needed to get put back on track, but other times it felt like she was taking her frustration out on me.

There were times my mother would come into our bedroom at 2 a.m. on a school night and make us get up to clean our closet. The closet always had things shoved in it, mostly dirty clothes, because our washing machine didn't work, which sometimes led to us pulling out dirty clothes to wear to school the next day. Other times, we washed our clothes in the tub with Ivory soap or dishwashing liquid, then hung them to dry. We'd place an old newspaper on the floor to absorb the water as the clothes dripped dry, or if we needed it quickly, we hung them on a hanger in front of the hot open oven. If our iron was broken, we cut the cord, sat it on the stove until it got hot, then ironed our clothes. Unfortunately, I burned a few holes in some of my clothes because the iron was too hot.

Memories of My Father

My father's name is Alex. Growing up, my mother always said, "You look like your no-good ass father!" Hearing those words caused me to immediately drop my head. I felt bad about looking like him and couldn't understand why she got upset with me because of it. I remember hearing her tell a story about when she was eight months pregnant with me. She and her cousin Sharon bumped into my father and another woman at a gas station. My mother got out of the car to confront him and noticed the other woman had a belly as big as hers. They were both pregnant. She said she was "so pissed off" her cousin had to stop her from "whooping his ass!"

I didn't see my father much growing up. There were a couple of times when he picked me up and brought me to visit his family. I can remember hearing laughter, calypso music, and the smell of Caribbean food in the air. Sometimes they spoke their native language, Spanish, and I'd just look up wondering what they were talking about. My aunties, Debbie and Arla, looked after me when I was there. They made sure I was bathed, fed and comfy before getting in bed.

My most memorable moment with my father is when he visited me after I got a third-degree burn while playing with my brother and godsister. We were sitting on the bed when my godsister said, "Let's see what will happen if we spray the deodorant towards the fire?" My brother lit the fire with a lighter, then she sprayed the deodorant towards the fire. All of a sudden, a huge fire ignited and burned my leg. Thank God the bed didn't go up in flames!

My godmother, Stella, who was asleep, woke up startled by the fire detector going off. I staggered over to her while holding the area that had been burned. Later, I was taken to the hospital, treated, and released.

My burn had to be cleaned every day. Whenever my mother prepared the cleaning solution, I cried hysterically because the burn was extremely painful. My mother was overwhelmed and frustrated with having to put up with my screaming and crying.

On a particular day while she was preparing to clean my burn, someone knocked on the door. It was my father. He came in the house, walked over to me, held my hand and stood right by my side. I remember holding onto his arm asking him to please help me. I wanted him to make my mother stop cleaning my burn or just take the pain away. That is the only memory I can recall having an emotional connection with him.

When I was ten years old, my father popped up to visit me again. He knocked on the door, grabbed my hand, and walked me downstairs. He said, "I want you to meet my wife." I was completely confused. It was almost as if he was speaking another language. I guess I was so surprised to see him, that it went right over my head. When we got downstairs, he walked me over to the car and said, "This is my wife, Cathy."

"Hello," I said. I didn't have much to say because I was a little shy, didn't know her, and barely knew him.

Not long after meeting Cathy, I started spending the weekends at their house. Cathy didn't have any children, so whenever my father was not home, we shopped, went to the hair salon, or I helped her cook. Cathy and I spent a lot of time together. She washed and pressed my hair and bought me new clothes. She always took the time to make sure I was pulled together. I'd talk a mile a minute if it were just Cathy and me, but as soon as my father came home, I wouldn't say much.

My father was not home most of the time, so I never got comfortable being around him. Whenever I said something to him, I

32

just started talking. I never called him daddy. After some time, he asked why I never called him daddy. I could tell it bothered him. He told me to start calling him daddy, but I had a hard time getting comfortable with it. Truthfully, I never developed a relationship with him and didn't get to know him as my father.

Risky Behaviors

Things were beginning to get out of control at my mother's house. At one point, a few drinks, and a pack of cigarettes were all she needed to satisfy her addiction. Later, I noticed more people coming in and out of the house on a regular basis. Because our bedroom was towards the back of the house, I couldn't see everyone, only a few people standing near the kitchen when I walked out of my room to go to the bathroom.

One evening, I noticed my mother and her friends cooking crack. Crack cocaine was heavily used during that time. I often saw empty vials tossed along the sidewalk when I played outside. Most times, it was sold in a small piece of plastic cut from a sandwich bag, then tied in a knot. I remember seeing them waiting eagerly as they held a glass tube or spoon over the fire on the stove. I also saw them smoking crack from a plastic bottle. The smell was different. It definitely didn't smell like marijuana. Once my mother started smoking crack, things started to quickly spiral downhill. Something didn't feel right. She was even more disconnected and could never stay still. She was always on the move.

When my brother, Gerard, was thirteen, he started a job selling candy in suburban communities with a group of neighborhood kids. The supervisor picked kids up and drove them out to the suburbs, where they went door-to-door selling chocolate-covered mints, peanut brittle, Katydids, and several other types of candy. Gerard loved his job because it gave him something positive to do while putting money in his pocket. Every night when he came home, he'd count his money, then stash it in a sneaker box. He saved all his money and sometimes gave me a dollar, but not often. Gerard wanted to save his money.

One Christmas, he bought me my very first pair of Guess jeans and Reebok sneakers. I LOVED my jeans and sneakers so much that I wore them at least two to three times each week. He also purchased a colored television for our room. It felt so good being able to watch Saturday morning cartoons like "Tom & Jerry, The Smurfs, and He-Man."

Sadly, one day he came home after work and noticed someone had stolen all his hard-earned money. He was so hurt and angry. I was upset as well because I knew how hard he worked for his money. A few weeks later, we came home from school; our television was gone. We believe it was sold for drugs. Although my brother was fed up with living under those conditions, he still continued to work and save his money.

One evening, while my brother was at work, I was lying down in our room watching television. My mother and her friends were hanging out drinking and using drugs. All of a sudden, I looked up and saw my mother's boyfriend's brother standing in the doorway.

"Hey Lee Lee," he said.

I said, "Hi."

He walked towards me and leaned over to give me a kiss. I turned my face in the other direction to avoid him kissing me on my lips. He grabbed my chin and forced my lips towards his, then put his tongue in my mouth. I was disgusted. I felt violated. I didn't even know this man. I knew what he had done was not right. I was nervous as I waited for him to leave so I could tell my mother. After he left, I told her what happened. She started cursing and yelling loudly and was ready to fight.

I sometimes wonder what could have happened if she had been outside with friends and he came up to use the bathroom. If he was bold enough to kiss me inappropriately with others in the next room, God only knows what he would have done if no one else was in the house.

Making Money

When I was almost twelve years old, I decided I wanted to get a job and make some money. I was tired of not having two pennies in my pocket to rub together or not being able to afford a new shirt or shoes. Gerard was bringing home money every weekend and I wanted to make some as well. There was an ice cream shop in Grove Hall named "Yours 40 Flavors." It was owned by a woman who lived in the community.

I stopped in to buy bubble gum ice cream from time to time and decided to ask if they were hiring. They were, and I was so excited! The only thing was you had to be at least fourteen years old to work there. They didn't ask for proof of age, so I did the math and completed the application. I got the job and started working that summer. Because of my job, I couldn't do everything my friends were doing that summer because most times I had to work. That was fine, though. I was just happy to be making money and having the freedom to buy some of the things I wanted.

While I was at work, a few of my friends came to buy some ice cream. One of them asked me to "hook her up" and put an extra scoop on her cone. Without question, I loaded her cone up with ice cream. After she left, the owner said, "If you ever do that again, I will take it out of your check!" That was all I needed to hear. I certainly did not want that to happen. I told my friends I could not "hook them up" anymore because I was not going to risk losing my job.

Later, I got a job working for Action for Boston Community Development (ABCD). This agency provided summer jobs for youth in the community. The goal of the program was to keep kids off the streets by giving them something productive to do while earning money. My first job was cleaning up the community with a team of other youth. The program was named "Red Shirts." Every day we reported to a specific location wearing our red shirts. When we got there, we loaded up the van with weed wackers, trash bags, gloves, and water. We'd ride to an open field in the neighborhood, get out the van, then start cleaning. The fields were filled with overgrown grass and trash. Sometimes we came across used drug needles and crack bottles. As the day went on, it got hotter and hotter, but we worked through it. Even though we had several breaks during the day, we'd try to venture off and hide to get a break. That experience was exactly what I needed to figure out what I didn't want to do ever again.

Fighting

My mother was a fighter. She would pop you in your lip so fast you wouldn't even know it was coming. Maybe that's why she ended up in a relationship with an abuser. Her boyfriend worked during the week and eventually started staying overnight. He bought the alcohol, and they got drunk together. Once they started drinking, they'd start arguing, and they often fought. I'd cover my ears or hide in my closet behind bags of clothes to avoid hearing the commotion. Other times, I would leave my room, peek around the corner, and yell, "Stop!!!"

On several occasions, my mother wouldn't let him in the house, and he'd kick the door right off the hinges! My mother sometimes called the police, but most times, she just propped a piece of furniture against the door to keep it in place until management came the next day to repair it. I never slept well on those nights. I was afraid someone would come in through our broken door while we were asleep.

My mother finally got sick and tired of fighting with her boyfriend. So, she boiled a pot of hot water and threw it on him after he kicked the door in. I was not home that weekend, thank God.

He was admitted to the hospital. A few days later my mother was also hospitalized after a neighbor threw hot lye on her. The neighbor was upset because she thought her boyfriend and my mother had been flirting around.

I stayed with Cathy and my father while my mother was in the hospital. Cathy took me to visit her. While we were there, the nurse asked, "Do you miss your mother?"

I said, "No."

My mother later told me how much it hurt her feelings to hear me say that I didn't miss her. However, I really did miss my mother. I hated to see her in pain, but I didn't miss all of the chaos that was happening at home.

Home Visits

Social Services was still involved and started doing more home visits. Whenever they asked how things were going, I always said things were good. I didn't want to be taken away from my mother and placed in foster care. After they asked me, they'd ask my brother. He always told the truth, and I'd just look at him and think, "Why is he telling on Mummy?"

My brother carried a lot of the stress from all that was going on and eventually started having seizures. We were at home when he had his first seizure. My mother frantically rushed over to him, turned him on his side, then waited until it was done. I was so afraid and never wanted to be home alone with him out of fear of him having one and not knowing what to do. I hated seeing him

38

go through this. It made me so sad, but I couldn't do anything to help him.

During this time, in order to prevent social services from taking us, my mother was required to check herself into a detox program. Although it was tough for her, she did and was sober for a period of time. It was refreshing seeing her sober. She took me with her to run errands more often. I felt proud being in public with her.

My mother's Alcoholics Anonymous meetings sometimes required my brother and me to be home alone. On this particular day, I was in the bathroom cornrowing my hair in the mirror.

Suddenly, my brother yelled, "Lisa!"

I didn't know what was wrong, but something didn't feel right. So, I ran out of the house with no shoes on, down three flights of stairs, then started running down the street shouting "Help!" I looked up and my mother happened to be walking towards the house. I screamed, "Gerard needs help!" My mother ran as fast as she could to get to him. By the time we got back, he was on the floor.

"Why did you leave me, Lisa?" he said as he looked over at me.

"I'm sorry. I was scared."

I'm so glad he didn't injure himself. I probably would have carried that guilt throughout my childhood.

Removed from Home

I was walking home after school from the bus stop. A car pulled over next to me. I looked to see who it was. I was surprised to see my social worker, Judy. My brother was sitting in the front seat with a blank stare on his face. I looked at Judy and my brother puzzled because I wasn't sure what was going on.

"Lisa, get in the car!"

When I got in, Judy told me she was taking us to a foster home. She said Gerard called her because my mother had been drinking that day, and he was concerned about our safety. I guess my brother was fed up. Although my mother had gone to detox programs several times, she never stayed sober for long. There were several occasions when social services threatened to remove us from our home, but this time, it finally happened.

PART 3

I Am a Product of My Environment

LISA HENDERSON-CARTER

42

Home #1

We drove down three blocks and turned right onto Crawford Street. I was confused. This home was literally a five-minute walk back to my house. Even though it was in the same neighborhood, it felt like I had moved to a whole new community. There were big, beautiful homes on the street. We pulled up to a big white house. Judy parked, then took us in to meet our new foster family, Mr. and Mrs. Carruthers.

The Carruthers were an older couple, maybe in their late sixties or seventies. Mrs. Carruthers seemed stern but welcomed us into her home. When we walked in, we were introduced to the family. Then Mrs. Caruthers showed me to MY room. There was a full-size bed, a dresser with a mirror, and a couple of nightstands. I was so happy! This was the first time that I ever had my own room.

After we got settled, Judy said she would check on us the next day, then she left. That's when the reality of what just happened set in. Although being so close to home was comforting, I also worried about my mom and was concerned about how she was doing.

Mrs. Carruthers was an amazing cook. She raised her own chickens and often prepared them for dinner. She had a deep freezer where she kept frozen foods and an extra refrigerator in the pantry area; both had chains and locks on them.

They had a big family who spent a lot of time together. Her granddaughter, Tracy, was my age and visited often. When we met, we clicked immediately. Several days a week, we went to the local Boys and Girls Club, where we practiced with the cheerleading team and hung out. One day, we decided to try to pull a fast one and left the club early to hang out with some guy friends we met at the club. We thought we had our story together. But, when we got home, we were separated into two different rooms and questioned. It didn't take long before Mrs. Carruthers realized our story did not add up. We were punished and not allowed to go back to the Boys and Girls Club for a while.

About a month later, Mrs. Carruthers requested that I be placed in another home. She didn't want to deal with the drama that came with having a preteen girl. My brother was allowed to stay, but I moved in temporarily with my new middle school friend, Kim, and her family. I had mixed emotions about moving. I didn't know when I'd see my brother again, but I had to leave. A part of me felt that Mrs. Carruthers was overreacting and didn't really give me a chance. The other part of me was happy to move in with Kim's family because they treated me like I was a part of their family.

Home #2

I met Kim at Mary E. Curley Middle School. It was the first day of school, and everyone in the sixth grade seemed to feel the same — out of place. Kim was in my class. She introduced herself to me, and that was all it took. From that point on, we started talking and became close friends. Kim lived near my house. When I lived with my mother, I would catch the #44 Humboldt bus and would arrive at her house in five minutes. Most times, I saved my quarter and walked to her house instead of riding the bus.

Kim had an older sister, Felisha, and a younger brother, Roy. Her parents, Mr. & Mrs. Harrison, accepted me into their home like I was their own. They allowed me to go in the refrigerator to fix something to eat, usually a bologna and cheese sandwich. But whenever we went into the kitchen, we "betta had washed our dirty hands!"

Mrs. Harrison always kept a clean house and expected us to clean up after ourselves. They had a system in their household. There was a day set aside to wash clothes, dry, and iron. I used to sit on the bed and watch Kim get all of her things cleaned and organized as she stomped through the house with her lips pouted out! Kim's dad, Mr. Harrison, was meek, low key and didn't say much. There were times we'd come in after engaging in "extracurricular activities" and hoped he was the one downstairs to greet us. We'd slide in, say hello, wash our hands, then keep moving to the kitchen. Mrs. Harrison, on the other hand, was more up close and personal. We couldn't "get over" with her, and now that I think about it, we weren't getting over with Mr. Harrison either. He saw everything but didn't say anything.

It was the beginning of summer in 1988 when I moved in with Kim's family. Kim and I had just completed the sixth grade. Her older sister, Felisha, didn't have to stay close to the front stoop, so we sometimes asked if we could hang out with her. Hanging with

45

Felisha gave us more freedom, but it also exposed us to risky behaviors and older guys. We were young, new to the game, and enjoying our freedom. On the other hand, the older guys knew the game and took advantage of our vulnerability.

One day, my social worker, Judy, asked Kim's parents if they would consider allowing me to stay permanently. Becoming my foster parent meant going through a full background check and being fully vetted by the Department of Social Services to ensure there were no concerns. Mrs. Harrison didn't mind me staying, but she did not want to deal with the red tape of having social services involved. So, once again, I had to pack my bags and move, but the Harrisons always kept an open door for me to visit.

Home # 3:

By this point, my father and Cathy had gotten divorced and she had remarried a man named Jimmy. Even though she remarried, she still checked in on me periodically. One afternoon, Cathy picked me up to spend the day with me. While driving down the street, she looked over and said, "There goes your father." I immediately felt a knot in my stomach. I wondered how he would feel knowing I was still connected to his ex-wife. Cathy pulled over next to my father and we got out of the car.

My father looked over at me and said, "What, are you pregnant?"

I was completely at a loss for words. "No," I said. I couldn't even understand why he asked something like that. I remember feeling so low. This man was my father, but he treated me like a complete stranger. They talked for a little while before we got back in the car. After we pulled off, there was complete silence for a moment. I was so angry about his response that I couldn't hold back my thoughts about him. Cathy listened and allowed me to openly express my feelings.

I ended up moving to Franklin Field Projects with my god-mother, Stella, and her daughter, Stephanie. This was my third move in less than three months, and I was beginning to feel over-whelmed by all of the changes. Stella had a two bedroom, so I shared a room with Stephanie. I did my best not to invade her space and tried to make the most of it, but I usually felt like I was in her way.

Chez Vous

That summer, I spent a lot of time with my girls from around the way. Every weekend we went roller skating at Chez Vous, our neighborhood skating rink. Chez Vous was the one place kids could easily get to by bus or walking within a couple of miles. We looked forward to going because it was one of the only places we could go without having to show proof of our age. The DJ always played the latest hip hop and R&B music. We always had a good time skating to the beat of the music and hanging out with our friends, especially if a fight didn't break out.

On Saturday nights, the rink was always packed. My girls and I would talk on the phone about our plans for the weekend. Some-times, we coordinated matching outfits, jean overalls, Adidas, or a fresh, clean pair of classic white Reeboks' and a bang with a ponytail to the side with ribbons or a bandana tied around it. I'd perm my edges, then use gel to slick my "baby hair" down. Going to "The Vouz" was always something we looked forward to.

At the end of the night, the last few songs were for couples only. Some people were already "booed up," while others sat and waited for someone to ask them to skate. We turned down an invite to skate if we weren't "feeling" the person who asked. We'd say, "No, thank you," or "I'm tired, my feet hurt." But man! If the right one asked, it was going down! All the way down.

Tender "Roni"

Chez Vous is where I met Coco. I could tell he was a regular at Chez Vous by the way he walked in, looked around, put on his skates, then smoothly eased his way onto the skating rink. He seemed confident and was well known, especially with the ladies. I saw him around a few times, but this time he came over during a couples only song and asked me to skate. I popped up without hesitation. He looked me in my eyes, took my hand, and we skated to slow jams. I immediately felt connected to him.

I was twelve years old, just one month shy of my thirteenth birthday. I told him I was a couple of years older, as most girls did. He was a few years older than me, and I must admit, he was pretty smooth with his game. He definitely was not new to this. We exchanged numbers and started talking on the phone and hung out after we left the skating rink.

Something about him made me feel safe and wanted. Whenever we hung out, he held my hand as we walked down the street and always made sure I walked on the inside of the sidewalk "so he could protect me." It didn't take long before one thing led to the other. We spent more time together and started doing grown-up things, which led to grown-up consequences.

The Results

For some reason, I had a feeling I was pregnant. I mentioned it to my mental health counselor, Rachel, who I recently started receiving therapy from after we were removed from my mother's custody. Rachel was the first adult I talked to about the possibility of being pregnant. She worked at the Codman Square Health Center, which was a neighborhood clinic that provided medical and mental health services for the community. Therapy was a mandatory part of my treatment plan, and although I didn't think it was necessary, it was what I needed.

At first, I didn't talk much, but meeting with her actually started to feel good. I enjoyed having a scheduled time to "get away from it all" and share my feelings with someone who had a non-judgmental ear. Rachel knew I had recently met my boyfriend. She listened intently whenever I shared anything about him. When I told her about the possibility of being pregnant, she immediately referred me to the clinic downstairs to take a pregnancy test. It was positive.

When I left my appointment, I walked back home slowly, thinking about everything. I had no idea if I was going to share the news with anyone. I certainly knew I wasn't going to tell my god-mother because she would tell my social worker, who would have been terribly disappointed, but not surprised.

It Takes Two to Tangle

When I got home, I called to tell my boyfriend the results. "I'm pregnant."

"For real?" he said in a calm voice. I could almost see him smiling through the phone. He didn't seem shocked at all.

"I don't know what to do," I said. I felt like one big ball of confused emotions.

"Well, are you going to keep the baby? I really want you to keep the baby," he said. "I'll be there to help you take care of our child."

A part of me wanted to believe him, but I was uncertain. I knew I had the right to make the final decision but making that kind of decision at this point in my life was more than I could handle. "I don't know what I'm going to do," I told him. But one thing I did know for sure was I needed to keep it a secret until I figured it out.

Keeping my pregnancy a secret was stressful. I told some of my friends who were already sexually active or lost their virginity soon after. So, it wasn't an uncomfortable conversation to have with them. They asked me what I was going to do. Even though we were within the same age range, they would say things like, "We'll help you," or "You all are gonna have a cute baby!" It was comforting knowing they *had my back*, but I also wondered what others would think of me, including their parents.

It wasn't long before Stella and Judy got the word. Although it was a relief knowing it was no longer a secret, I was then faced with dealing with their opinions and thoughts. Stella didn't say much. I believe she felt stuck in the middle. Judy said it was best for me not to keep the baby and suggested I put the baby up for adoption.

My mother got the news shortly after the word got out. I can only imagine what she must have felt knowing I had JUST been removed from her care, and now, THIS! My mother reached out and planned a day to talk with me. I didn't know what to expect because growing up, I didn't spend much quality time with her. We met at an eat-in fast food restaurant in Washington Park mall. I ordered chicken tenders and fries. Then we sat down to eat at a small table.

My mom looked at me and asked, "What do you want to do?"

"I don't know," I said and looked at her with shame-filled eyes. I hated having to have this conversation with her.

"I'm not going to make you have an abortion because you won't hate me for the rest of your life!" she said.

Honestly, I was surprised by her response. I expected her to be angry, after all, she did tell me, *"Nothing should go between my legs but a washcloth and some soap."* Clearly, that didn't happen. Although I had a few close calls with boys when I lived with her, there was something about the THOUGHT of her finding out that quickly made me think about the consequences I would have received from my mother.

Pediatrics

I scheduled an appointment with my pediatric physician, Dr. Siegel, to discuss my results. He had been my doctor since birth. I loved going to my annual physicals with my mother because it was one of the things that was consistent in my life. The nurses were always friendly and made the experience fun. Getting my weight and height measured, having my temperature taken, and passing my hearing and vision screenings gave me a feeling of fulfillment. Whenever Dr. Siegal came into the room when I was young, he'd greet us, ask how things were going, then ask a bunch of questions about my overall health. At the end of my appointment, he'd tell me how well I was doing and how smart I was, then I'd receive a sticker and a lollipop, which always put a smile on my face.

This appointment was different, though. Although I was still young enough to receive pediatric care, I needed to share "big girl" news with him this time. Dr. Siegel walked in the exam room and greeted me with a smile.

"Hi! How are you? What brings you in today?"

"I'm pregnant," I said and dropped my head. I was ashamed. I could see the look of concern in his eyes as he looked at the little girl he had taken care of since birth. He talked with me for a little while, then informed me that I needed to see a prenatal doctor. My heart dropped at the thought of seeing a different doctor. After all, Dr. Siegel knew me. He knew my history and the challenges my family experienced. I was devastated, but I understood. I understood my decisions were changing the dynamics of my entire life.

New School

During my sixth-grade year, students were given the opportunity to take an examination test for admission into the Boston Latin School (BLS), one of the most prestigious exam schools in Boston. I passed the test and now was able to receive an education from one of THE best college preparatory schools. I was so excited when I found out I scored high enough to attend and looked forward to enrolling in the fall. However, much had transpired in my life in a short period of time since receiving my test scores:

1. I was placed in DSS custody.

2. I moved to three different homes within three months.

3. I recently got the results of my pregnancy test.

I started seventh grade at Boston Latin School a few weeks after receiving the results of my pregnancy test. Judy was concerned about my future and how having a baby at thirteen could potentially destroy my life. Not only did I have pressure from those closest to me about whether or not to keep the baby, I also had to deal with the opinions of those at my new school.

My new school was within walking distance from Boston Children's and Beth Israel Hospital in Boston. Every day, I walked from Franklin Field projects to Blue Hill Avenue to catch the bus to Dudley Station. Once I got to Dudley, there was a bus just for students that took us directly to school without stopping at every bus stop. Dudley was where kids from every neighborhood met before they went to school, while others just hung out there. The mornings were usually low key, but the afternoons were when fights typically broke out. Police officers were always patrolling the area, but that didn't stop the kids from meeting there to fight with someone after school. Some people would hang around to watch, while others kept it moving, just trying to make it back home.

Being a seventh grader and pregnant at Boston Latin was challenging. The thought of "one of their students having a baby" was not the reputation they wanted. A conference was scheduled at the school to talk with me about my plans. When I walked into the conference room, there was a room full of adults. My social worker, the school nurse, the counselor, my teachers, and the school administrators all sat on one side of the room. I noticed there was a chair for me on the other side. I felt intimidated and didn't know what to expect.

Sitting there was like watching a scene from a movie as I listened to multiple voices in the room.

"Do you want to end up like your mother, on welfare and using drugs?" one person asked.

"Having a baby can influence other students to do the same," someone else stated.

"You're going to end up dropping out of school."

My heart filled up with so many emotions, emotions of fear and uncertainty. I finally broke my silence. With tears running down my face, I screamed, "I'll have an abortion!" I knew I didn't want to end up like my mother, on welfare and using drugs and alcohol. All I wanted was to enjoy being a kid, hanging out with my friends, bus rides through Dudley, and getting an education so I could be successful.

My Decision

After the meeting at school, I scheduled an appointment to have an abortion. I was just beginning to have morning sickness. Throwing up several times a day was taking a toll on my fragile body. As the day approached, I had so many mixed emotions. I wish I didn't even have to deal with this whole situation.

When I arrived, a nurse prepared me for the procedure and propped my feet up in the stirrups. The doctor came in, sat down, then picked up an instrument to start the procedure. All of a sudden, I felt an overwhelming feeling come over me. I abruptly sat up and said, "I don't want to do this!"

The doctor immediately stopped, and said, "Thank you for saying something." He called in a family planning counselor who listened and supported me through my decision. She talked about the next steps and the importance of getting prenatal care to ensure I had a healthy pregnancy and baby. Although I had no idea what the future would hold for my unborn child and me, I felt a sense of peace because a decision had been made.

I was referred to the Teen and Tot Clinic for prenatal care, which was on the same floor as the Pediatrics clinic. My boyfriend went with me to my appointment. I remember sitting in the waiting room looking around at other teens who were expecting babies; some already had children.

I met my nurse practitioner, Mrs. Ramsey. I immediately felt comfortable with her. She was like the auntie most families in the African American community had. She was down to earth, had a great sense of humor, and told you what you needed to hear, not what you wanted to hear! Her experience and sincere interest in the field of providing care for adolescents were evident. I always kept my medical appointments because I was interested in knowing how my baby was developing, but mostly because she expected me to take responsibility for my health. I was thirteen, but my decision to have my baby put me in a totally different category. I now had to think and make decisions like an adult.

Alternative School

Although being pregnant was not well received at Boston Latin, I attended until I was asked to transition to St. Margaret's, an alternative school for pregnant teens. I was about six months pregnant when I left. Leaving was yet another reality that hit me in the face. I didn't quite understand why being pregnant made a difference. After all, I went to school every day and did my best to keep up with my assignments. I was told it was best for me to go to an alternative school for safety reasons. The school didn't want to be responsible if something happened to me while I was there. It didn't make sense to me, but I had no other option, so I left and went to St. Margaret's.

The alternative school was an extension of a small hospital, which I never knew existed. My new school was located in a little house with brown wooden floors and a few desks. There were about four other girls who attended as well. Something about going to school made me feel isolated from everyone. We all sat in a room working on packets of printed assignments. There was a teacher there to answer questions if we needed help, but other than that, I don't remember learning much.

After leaving class, I went home, ate something, then called my friends to see how their day went at school. I couldn't wait to go back to regular school, but my baby was not due until May. Therefore, I had to finish out the school year there.

Preterm Labor

About a month after I started attending St. Margaret's, I began experiencing preterm labor symptoms and was hospitalized. A procedure was performed where a long needle was stuck into my stomach to test the amniotic fluids to see if the baby's lungs were developed. The doctor determined they weren't fully developed. So, they gave me a steroid treatment to speed up the process. My boyfriend was there with me most days and slept on a hospital cart in my room. He was concerned about the baby and me. Even though he tried his best to be supportive, I still felt alone. I felt alone and was very concerned because I didn't know what was about to happen to my unborn child or me. I had to trust that the doctors and nurses would take care of us.

I stayed in the hospital for almost two weeks. While there, I received a call that my mom was admitted into the Intensive Care Unit at the same hospital. My brother, who I hadn't seen since we were separated, had also gotten the call. He visited her before coming to see me. When he walked into the room, I said, "Hi Gerard, how's mummy?" He looked perplexed. "I want to go see her," I said.

"I don't think that's a good idea. She doesn't look good," he said.

"Ok, I'll wait until she gets out of the hospital." I trusted my brother and figured it was best for me to wait, especially considering the health issues I was having myself.

Later, my boyfriend came to visit me and said he had a chance to visit my mother. He also said she didn't look good and had told him to please take care of me.

A few days later, I was released from the hospital and placed on bed rest for the duration of my pregnancy. Stella made me stay home and fussed when I asked if I could go anywhere. It was hard staying in the house, so I called my friends and we talked on the phone. Sometimes they would stop by the house before heading out to do what most teens were doing, having a good time! Seeing them leave while I stayed at home was hard. I'd watch them from the window as they walked away laughing loudly. I wished I could join them, but instead I yelled out the window, *"Ya'll have fun!"*

PART 4

I AM SURVIVING

The Call

My mother was still in the intensive care unit and couldn't accept any phone calls. About a week or so after I was released from the hospital, the phone rang at about 5 a.m. I was asleep and wondered, *Who in the world is calling this early?* I figured someone must have had the wrong number if they were calling THAT early in the morning. Not giving it much thought, I fell back to sleep, but was awakened a couple of hours later by my godmother.

"Lisa!" she yelled.

"Yes?"

"Come and get the phone."

I slowly got out of the bed, waddled down to her room, then took the phone. It was Judy.

"Lisa, your mom died."

I stood there for a moment thinking, "Did I just hear what I thought I heard?" After processing what she said, I felt like I couldn't breathe. I gasped for air, threw the phone down, then screamed out as tears ran down my face. I didn't expect her to die. I expected her to get better. My hope was that she'd stop drinking and using drugs, and we'd eventually go back home. I didn't believe it! I just could not believe it.

So later that night, I called the hospital to check in on her. The receptionist said, "She expired." I called several more times but kept getting the same response over and over again. I couldn't understand why they used the term "expired." To me, that word meant something was no longer any good, but in this case, it meant my mother was gone. It meant I wouldn't see her again. It meant I'd stay in foster care. It meant she would never meet her grandchild. I was devastated.

The Funeral

A few days later, Stella took me to buy something to wear to the funeral. I was eight months pregnant and needed something big enough to go over my stomach. She found a navy-blue dress and a pair of navy-blue shoes.

The day I dreaded finally arrived, the day of my mother's funeral. I had a strange feeling throughout my whole body. I was nervous. Losing my mother was beginning to feel real. The service was held at J.B. Johnson's Funeral Home, a well-known local funeral home in the heart of Roxbury. It was a small family-owned mortuary located in a two story, white house. The small chapel seated about thirty people. Others stood along the walls or paid their respect, and then left.

When I walked in, there were quite a few people there. I felt like all eyes were on me. I could hear voices, saying, "There goes Lee Lee." Some family and friends came to give me a hug. I barely saw anyone's face, but I could sense that they were thinking, "Oh, my goodness, she's pregnant!"

I sat in the front row next to my brother, uncle, and other family members. We were only a few feet away from the casket. I held my head down because I was afraid to see my mother lying there. Every now and then, I'd look up to see other people's responses as they walked up to view her body. Many shook their heads, then walked away with tears in their eyes.

This was my first funeral. I didn't know what to expect. I certainly didn't want to see my mother in this state. After the eulogy, the family had the opportunity to say their final goodbyes.

I couldn't get up the nerve to walk over to the casket to say goodbye. I was afraid. Someone came over to help me get up. They slowly walked me towards her. I stood there in disbelief. I looked at her for a while. She had on a curly wig and a flower-patterned dress. Although my mother was a fair-skinned woman, her complexion appeared blotchy and dark. I stared at her, thinking she would open her eyes, but she didn't. My heart was crushed. I was in disbelief seeing her laying there. How could I accept that my mummy was gone?

Suddenly, I felt dizzy and the next thing I remember was hearing a lot of background noise, but one voice stood out above the rest; it was Jimmy's voice, Cathy's new husband.

"EVERYONE, MOVE OUT OF THE WAY! She needs air!" he shouted.

When I came to, I looked over and saw Jimmy and Cathy right by my side. They helped me get up, then walked me outside to the family car.

I sat there, numb with images of my mother laying in that casket. We waited until everyone came out of the funeral home. Then the family car followed the hearse to the burial site. I stared out the window as we drove through the neighborhood I grew up in and past the building we lived in. I recalled memories of playing outside and seeing mummy walking to the store.

Throughout the entire funeral, I could feel my baby kicking inside of me, but I felt totally disconnected. I was consumed with concern about my mother. I wondered if she could breathe closed in that casket. I wondered if she was yelling and pleading for someone to let her out. These thoughts flooded my mind throughout the ride. Occasionally, I'd glance over at my brother and my mother's youngest brother, Uncle Darry, and wonder what they were thinking. My brother didn't say anything, though. He just looked straight ahead with a blank stare on his face.

When we arrived at the cemetery, we got out of the car, then walked through the rocky gravel to her burial site. After the final remarks were said, the funeral director handed me a yellow carnation. As we were driving away, I looked back towards my mother's grave and felt so sad because we were leaving her all alone.

My mother was only thirty-three years old when she died. She still had been drinking heavily and using crack cocaine before she died. As a matter of fact, her usage increased after me and my brother were removed from our home. Her drug and alcohol abuse killed her. She literally poisoned her system and eventually suffered from cardiac arrest.

The Delivery

Losing my mother was traumatic, but I didn't have a chance to grieve. Instead, I was going to my weekly prenatal appointments, preparing to have my baby, and focused on completing school assignments, while on bed rest.

A few weeks later, I started experiencing labor pains. These were different from the ones I had felt before. So, I told Stella, but she said I was fine. She must have known I wasn't fully in labor and didn't want to risk being sent back home from the hospital.

Later that evening, the pain increased and was unbearable. I went to her room and laid next to her twisting from side to side in agony. I begged her to take me to the hospital. The pain intensified, and I started to cry. At that point, she knew I was finally in labor. She finally called the ambulance, and I was rushed to the hospital.

When we arrived, my boyfriend met us there and stayed by my side the entire time. The nurses hooked me up to a monitor to track my contractions and the baby's heart rate. I could hear the swishing sound of my baby moving around as he prepared to enter the world. The doctors and nurses were in and out of the room, checking to see how much I dilated. This process seemed like it was never going to end. At one point, I didn't think I was going to make it. It was as if life and death flashed right before my thirteen-year-old eyes. I cried out in pain. I eventually asked for medication to help with the pain.

"Honey, you're too far along to have an epidural," the nurse said. "You can do this. I need you to breathe."

"I don't think I can do this," I said through clenched teeth as tears rolled down my cheeks.

The nurse kept encouraging me, "You're almost there. You can do this!"

I thought I wasn't going to make it. I didn't think my thirteen-year-old body was capable of bringing forth a child.

Shortly after, the doctor came in and told me it was time to push. Hearing those words was like music to my ears. All I knew was I needed that baby out of me! After a few pushes, I could hear the cry of my child. He was a healthy, beautiful, baby boy who weighed seven pounds, three ounces, and had a head full of hair. I couldn't believe I was holding MY child. I stared at him as I cuddled him in my arms. He had chubby cheeks and all his fingers and toes.

My son was born exactly one month from the date my mother died. For some reason, holding him made me feel connected to her. It was almost as if she wanted to let me know I'd be ok. I had doubts, though. I wanted to give him the very best, but I was not prepared and had no idea what it meant to be a mother. All I knew was I had a responsibility on my hands bigger than anything I ever experienced.

After we were discharged from the hospital, my new reality hit me like a sack of bricks. Taking care of a baby was something no one could have ever prepared me for. Waking up every two hours to feed, burp, and change his diaper was exhausting. My godmother helped me every now and then, but he was my baby and my responsibility. His dad came by often to spend time with us, but when he left, I was still there with our baby.

Can I Live?

A few weeks later, I started experiencing postpartum depression. Losing my mother, having a baby, and being sleep-deprived were all beginning to catch up with me. Also, the reality of having to stay home to take care of a baby, my baby, and not being able to hang out with my friends was getting the best of me. I was beginning to resent my boyfriend because he still hung out with his friends while I was stuck in the house.

One day all my emotions came crashing down. I just couldn't take it anymore. I felt so hopeless, so lost. I decided I didn't want to live anymore. I looked at my innocent baby as he slept in his crib, leaned over, gave him a kiss, then told him how much I loved him.

Then, I picked up my prescription strength pain pills, opened the bottle, then swallowed a handful. After taking the pills, I sat down and immediately regretted my decision. I didn't want my son to grow up without a mother. He needed me! I wanted to live. I was so conflicted because I felt helpless and wanted the pain to go away. I didn't know where to turn or what to do. Shortly after, my heart began to race, and I panicked. I needed to let someone know what I had done, so I rushed to the phone and called a medical professional.

"You need to call the poison control center immediately," the voice on the other end of the phone said sternly.

Instead of calling the poison control center, I laid down and closed my eyes, hoping, somehow, I'd wake up. A couple of hours later, I woke up to the baby crying. When I opened my eyes, I felt weak, but I was alive. With gratitude, I picked up my baby, prepared his bottle and fed him with a strength beyond myself.

Saving Grace

My boyfriend's paternal grandmother, Ma, was my saving grace. She loved my son, and always welcomed us into her home and treated me with respect. She didn't allow any "hanky panky" in her house and expected bedroom doors to stay open, which I fully respected. Every time we visited, she had something cooking on the stove, and I knew we'd have a good home-cooked meal with a tall glass of ice-cold lemonade or iced tea. Sometimes she made smothered pork chops with gravy and rice, chicken, or spaghetti. I loved everything she cooked. Her meals were always made with love.

Ma would take the baby while I sat at the table to eat. She'd smile and play with him, then look over and say, "That porkchop is tough," or "That spaghetti didn't come out right." Meanwhile, I'd be throwing down, enjoying every bite. Ma didn't say much. Most times, you could hear her humming a melody in the background. She was a hard-working woman who worked every day, went to the grocery or thrift store, then came home to cook, clean, and take care of her family.

Ma knew I was in a tough situation. So, sometimes she kept my son overnight so I could have a weekend to myself. Losing my mother and being in the foster care system was difficult enough, let alone taking care of a baby. I knew my son was in good hands when he was with Ma. She made sure he was safe, fed, and loved.

Back To School

I returned to Boston Latin that fall to begin my eighth-grade year, but was informed the credits I earned from the alternative school did not meet the requirements for promotion. I was so upset and thought, *How in the world could I be kept back when I successfully finished the program?* I felt betrayed. It was at that moment I realized I was being held liable for my decision to have my baby. I didn't feel supported and decided to go to my assigned school. After all, having a student with a baby was not the reputation Latin school wanted to have anyway.

I was assigned to the Grover Cleveland in Dorchester, MA, where once again, I had to adjust to being in a new environment. Being the "new kid on the block" was annoying because some of the girls felt like they had to prove a point by trying to size me up. They'd stare at me with their lips turned up like I did something to them! There was something about my presence they didn't like. Maybe it was the attention I got from boys or their curiosity about who I was and where I came from.

Word soon got around that I had a baby. I started hearing whispers, "She has a baby!" I didn't let it stop me from doing what I was there to do, but I made it clear that I was NOT the one to mess around with. I didn't start trouble, but I definitely knew how to handle any that came my way. Whenever I walked down the hall, I'd look them straight in their eyes with a look that said, "*Please, don't try me.*" I had no time for games. I was in school to get my education.

As a young mother, I had to think twice about my response to people who tried to intimidate or test me. I'd ask myself if it was really worth it? I didn't always make the best choices when it came to dealing with drama. I even had situations that could have landed me in jail, but I am grateful my conscience always led me back to my values; respect for others and wanting more for my future. I learned how to smile right through those challenging times, because after all, I had enough on my own plate to deal with.

Big Sister

After having my son, Judy, signed me up to receive a mentor through the Big Brothers Big Sisters program. During my initial interview, I was asked a series of questions about my likes and dislikes. I was also asked if it mattered if my mentor was white or black. I paused for a moment and thought, *I'd prefer if she was black*, but I thought that would have been rude. So, instead, I said, "It doesn't matter."

Several weeks later, I met my big sister, Erika, and my first thought was, *"Well, I did say 'it didn't matter' about her race."* Erika was a young white woman in her mid-twenties. Every other week, she would visit or take me out for a ride in her burgundy Honda Accord.

In the beginning, I felt uncomfortable and didn't want to be seen driving in my neighborhood with her because I felt like all eyes were on me. As we started developing a relationship, it didn't matter as much, and I really didn't care who saw me. She was MY big sister, and I knew she cared about me.

The first few times we got together, she took me to my favorite place to eat, McDonald's. Although she wasn't a huge fan of McDonald's, she was willing to go where I wanted to go. We sat and talked about how things were going and my hopes and dreams. Some of my dreams were to go to school for nursing, move my son away from the violence, buy a Honda Accord, and one day own a home. I was able to openly share my thoughts with Erika. When we talked, I actually felt as though my dreams could become a reality.

After we got to know one another, she invited my son and me to her home. We baked cookies and carved pumpkins. Sometimes, we ate dinner together at the dinner table, which was uncommon for me. We'd set the table, sit down together, then pray before eating. Erika's husband, Robin, sometimes joined us. Robin was a gentle soul and accepted us into his home. They loved each other. I could tell by their interactions with one another. They greeted each other with a kiss, then asked about each other's day. They didn't have any children. However, they managed to find a place in their hearts to share their love with a complete stranger. That stranger was me, Lisa, and her son, Marlin, also known as "Mookie."

Erika knew I was grieving the loss of my mother but never pretended to imagine what it felt like. She was the first one to take me to visit my mom's gravesite. When we arrived at the cemetery, we were directed to my mother's plot by a staff member. Her plot was bare. Unfortunately, she didn't have a tombstone.

Shortly after, Erika bought materials so I could make a cross for my mother's gravesite. She took two planks of wood to make a cross, then gave me a tool to engrave a message for my mother. We placed the cross on her gravesite and bought her some flowers. I was so proud to be able to make and give my mom a gift, my handmade cross.

Erika was an angel sent from God. She didn't ask a lot of nosy questions. She just let our relationship develop authentically. Having her in my life gave me a glimpse of hope. I didn't realize it then, but years later, I was able to see how she was strategically placed in my life.

Chronic Asthma

I continued receiving medical care at the Teen & Tot clinic and my son received care at the Pediatric clinic. The provider I chose for my son was my former pediatrician, Dr. Siegal. Receiving care from Dr. Siegal was exactly what I needed to transition into parenthood. Dr. Siegal was supportive, thorough and always made me feel comfortable asking questions related to my son's health. I felt empowered.

My son struggled with respiratory issues and later started having frequent asthma attacks. He was prescribed several medications and eventually received an at-home nebulizer machine that I traveled with to ensure he received treatments every four to six hours. If he had a severe attack, he was hospitalized and prescribed steroids. I followed a strict order prescribed by the doctor in order to wean him off steroids slowly.

Even though he suffered from asthma, he was very active and ran around like the average child, so I had to keep a close eye on him. I could always tell when he was in distress by looking at his rib cage as he breathed in and out. His breaths were much faster and intense, but that didn't stop him from running up and down the hall; even the doctors couldn't figure out how his oxygen level could be so low, yet he was always vibrant and full of energy.

We spent so much time at the hospital, I knew exactly what to expect and was prepared to answer all of the questions related to his health. The doctor always asked, "Does anyone in the house smoke?" I'd answer with the same response every time, "Yes." Stella was aware of my son's health condition and started smoking in her room, but the smell of smoke still filled the air. I came home one day and could smell smoke. With frustration, I yelled, "Can you PLEASE stop smoking in the house?"

She looked at me and said, "This is my goddamn house!"

She was absolutely right. It was her house. I didn't have the right to tell her what to do. I realized the only thing I had control over was sharing my concerns. I talked with Judy about those concerns and we were moved to another foster home.

Moving away from my godmother's house was necessary for my son's health, but it was tough because it was a familiar place. I spent time there when I was a little girl, and I know she genuinely cared about me. She took me into her home and allowed me to stay even after getting pregnant and having a baby. I can't imagine the level of stress she must have experienced throughout my time there. Although she was always a smoker, I'm sure the extra responsibilities didn't help any.

Home #4

The next foster home I moved to was with a lady named Ms. Elizabeth. She lived in Brighton, MA, which was on the outskirts of the city, only one bus ride from my stomping ground and my boyfriend's house. The new foster parent laid out ALL the rules on the first day. She told me I could only go out every other day, and my curfew was at 5 p.m. She was very strict. Right away, I knew living there was going to be an issue. I felt like I was locked down, which was a hard adjustment from living with my godmother, where I had a lot more freedom.

One afternoon, I met my boyfriend so he could see his son. I knew I wasn't going to make my curfew, so I called to let her know I was running late. Ms. Elizabeth said, "Stay right where you are!" She told me social services needed to find another place for me to live because she wasn't going to be responsible if I got pregnant again. I called Judy to let her know, and she told me to go home. I went home, but not long after, we were moved to another home.

The new home was my fifth placement, so packing was not an issue. I was used to living out of trash bags and moving from place to place. I didn't allow myself to get comfortable. I soon developed a *"whatever happens, happens"* mentality. At the time, I couldn't understand why she was so strict, but now I understand. Being responsible for a baby with a baby was a bit much. Most foster parents didn't accept young parents for that reason, which made it tough for social services to find a home for us.

During this time, my social worker questioned my ability to take care of my son and mentioned the possibility of putting him in someone else's care. I didn't agree and was angry with her for even thinking about it. He was *my* child, and it was *my* responsibility to take care of him. Furthermore, his dad's family would not have allowed it without fighting in court to get custody of him. I didn't make the best choices, but if anyone took my son away from me, it may have impacted my mental stability in a way that would not have been good.

Relationship Issues

There were so many changes that took place in my life in such a short period of time that I didn't know if I was coming or going. Being placed in foster care, saying goodbye to my mother, and taking care of an innocent life that depended on me was overwhelming. My son's father was a few years older than me, and although he was excited about becoming a father, the reality of what that really meant was a different story. Being a new dad, trying to go to school, wanting to be young and hang out with his boys, all while being expected to find a job to help take care of his son, was his new life.

All of these factors showed how unprepared we were to take care of a baby. The relationship that was once a bed of roses quickly went south. I no longer felt butterflies in my stomach when he called or when we were together. I was just overwhelmed with the responsibility of taking care of my baby. I expected more from him. If I wanted to go out with my friends, I had to make arrangements, but he could come and go as he pleased. I felt like I had gotten the short end of the stick.

We started getting into arguments. Then gradually, our arguments turned into physical fights. Once the fighting began, the relationship took a turn for the worse. Growing up seeing my mother fight her boyfriend made it a natural response for me to fight back. As time went on, the fighting became regular. Whenever I threatened to break up with him, he'd say things like, "You have my son, and you're not going anywhere." I felt stuck and found myself staying on guard and prepared to defend myself, just in case. Eventually, I got tired of fighting and decided it was best not to be together.

One day, our son was admitted into the hospital for asthma. This was his fourth or fifth time being admitted, so it had become the norm. We had a private room with a chair that turned into a fold-out bed, a television, a bathroom, and a crib that resembled a metal cage.

My son's father came to visit him, but we were not on the best terms at the time. Before he left, he asked me about our relationship. I was fed up and tired of going through the motions. He must have sensed that I was not interested in being in a contentious relationship with him. Before I knew what was happening, he pulled out a gun and put it to my head.

With tears in my eyes, I looked over at my son in the crib, and said, "You might as well kill me." I was angry and couldn't believe he put a gun to my head in front of our son. Although my son was too young to understand what was happening, I understood. I knew I didn't want to be with someone who said they loved me but used fear as a tactic to keep me. Even more so, I was utterly disgusted that I had a child with someone who threatened my life, in a hospital room, next to our sick child.

Realizing his fear tactic didn't work, he grabbed his things, and quickly left. I couldn't believe what had just happened, but I knew I needed to report the incident. I called the nurse and told her what happened. She called the security guard to talk with me, but he said there was nothing they could do. I remember feeling helpless. I didn't know where things were going to end up with our relationship, but I knew in my heart I wasn't going to live in fear.

Home #5

After moving from Brighton, I ended up right back in my hood, where I grew up. My new foster parents, the Jacksons, lived right in between Grove Hall and Humboldt Avenue. Being back felt good because it was a familiar place. I reconnected with my girls, and we picked up right where we left off, hanging out and having a good time. The only issue was that I had an earlier curfew than my friends, but at least it was not at 5 p.m.!

In order to go to house parties, I would ask my foster mother if I could stay at my friend's house for the weekend. Every weekend there was something to get into. Most times, we went skating at Chev Vous, walked downtown to shop, or just hung out on the block. Other times, we went to house parties and stayed until 2 or 3 in the morning. We drank forty ounces of Private Stock, Heineken, or Cisco and smoked weed all night long. We laughed, got loud and rowdy, and sometimes had confrontations with girls from other neighborhoods.

Youth violence in Boston was at an all-time high in the '90s. There was always a "beef" with many of the surrounding rival gangs. Every block had to make a name and uphold their reputation for themselves. Even though we all lived in the same community, it was nothing to suddenly hear bullets from a drive-by while standing on the block or walking to the corner store. During that time, someone getting shot or stabbed was a regular occurrence. You just hoped it wasn't someone you knew. Most times, it was.

Once, I was walking down the street and heard gunshots coming from behind me. When I turned around, someone was aiming his gun at a person who was running directly towards me. All of a sudden, "something" told me to run in a zigzag motion. That's what saved me from getting shot because there was no other place to run. Thankfully, I didn't have my son with me at the time, which made it easier to run. God only knows what could have happened if he had been with me.

Through all the chaos, I still loved being back closer to home. We were family and looked out for each other. They loved my son and kept an eye on him like he was theirs. We experienced good times and bad times together. Although I have so many good memories, I felt a strong sense that I was at a crossroad. Because I grew up seeing my mother fight, I was a fighter. I also saw my mother drinking and using drugs. I, too, enjoyed drinking and smoking weed. I definitely loved partying and having a good time, like most teens did, but I also had a son who looked up to and depended on me.

While hanging out one day, my son cursed and said something inappropriate. It was gang-related and could have caused a lot of issues. Everyone laughed because they were shocked at what he said since he was only two years old. I was shocked, too, and chuckled initially, but I immediately felt a shift in me. I didn't want to raise a child who was disrespectful or ended up in jail or in a gang. I had to acknowledge that I allowed him to be exposed to certain things, and he was absorbing it like a sponge. I knew I had to make a change.

I later found out his dad taught him to say gang-related comments. I confronted him and told him I was not going to raise my son that way and didn't appreciate him teaching him to curse.

PART 5

I AM CREATING MY FUTURE

Crossroads

Not long after, my son's dad went to prison for a serious crime. I was fifteen years old and had just started high school at The English High School of Boston. English High had a teen parenting program that provided on-site childcare for students. Every day I got up and got us ready for school. Then a school bus picked us up from the house. When I arrived at school, I signed my son into daycare, got him settled, then went to class when the bell rang. In between classes, I was able to stop by and look through the big glass window to check in on him. He loved going to daycare, and they LOVED them some "Mookie," the nickname I gave him when he was born.

Every day they greeted him with the biggest smile and hug. I didn't have to worry about packing food because they served breakfast and lunch. They read books, sang songs, and took the children out for a walk during the day. His teachers were blown away by his ability to read words so early. I spent a lot of time reading books to him, and he LOVED reading books with me. His speech and language skills were more advanced than the average child, which was great, but also challenging because it took more effort to keep him engaged.

I was assigned a case manager through the teen parenting program. Her name was Angela. She met with me to discuss my goals, overall academic experience, and parenting concerns. Her office was located in the school, which made it easier to schedule and keep appointments or drop in if needed. Having her support was instrumental in helping me stay on track. There were other teen moms and dads who were also trying to finish school while parenting. However, most of the people I developed lasting friendships with didn't have children.

Having so many different types of friends was typical for me. I had friends from around the way I could call and wouldn't think twice about handling a problem if an issue needed to be resolved, friends who were college-bound, friends who came from single-parent homes, and friends who had both parents in the home. Every last one of them played a role in my life and served a purpose. All my friends loved my son and their love for me was shown through their love for him.

Being a student at English High, gave me the opportunity to be a teen parent and go to school with my friends. Although I went to school every day and maintained the honor roll, I had my share of poor decision-making that could have changed the trajectory of my life. It seemed like everyone in high school smoked weed or drank. We enjoyed it. It was one of our favorite pastimes. It wasn't until much later that I realized I needed to slow it down a bit.

While in high school, I was exposed to opportunities that opened the door for new experiences, including getting accepted into a paid medical program called ProTech. Because I had an interest in pursuing a nursing career (inspired by the many days I spent at the hospital with my son), this program was just what I needed. My job was in the Angiography department at Brigham and Women's Hospital, where I prepared patients for their procedures. I met so many wonderful people and had to put my best foot forward. I had a personalized name badge and wore scrubs like the doctors and nurses. I loved earning a check at the end of the week with MY name on it. It felt GOOD.

Not only did I work at the hospital, but I also participated in several different opportunities that exposed me to life beyond the streets, including being interviewed by USA Today about my experience as a teen parent and the impact the Teen Parenting Program had on me. Seeing me and my son's faces on the front page was yet another step in the direction of taking my "lemons and making lemonade."

Home #6

I moved once again–this time with my father's ex-wife, Cathy, and her husband, Jimmy. Cathy stayed in touch with me throughout my transition from foster home to foster home. She always expressed her concern for me, and the fact that Jimmy allowed us to move into their home was truly a blessing. I was too immature to understand then, but as an adult, I am often brought to tears just thinking about their heart and willingness to not only serve as foster parents, but as my parents. I had my share of ups and downs while there, but they showed grace and wanted me to succeed. I continued going to English High and developed a close relationship with a small group of girls who came from homes where their parents also expected them to do well in school. Having those friendships, like many others, was an important part of finishing school successfully.

I also experienced dealing with girls who didn't like me for whatever reason. I ignored it for as long as I could until I just had enough. I remember being upset for allowing someone to push me to the point of fighting and wanting it all to stop. When I got called to the office to discuss what happened, I was not suspended from school because I never got into trouble, and the staff knew it was out of character for me to fight at school. Having that level of support made me feel even more connected to my high school experience. Knowing I had a team that supported me was another reason for me to make better decisions.

I had to travel back and forth to school with my son, and because I no longer took a school bus, I had to pay closer attention to my surroundings when traveling via public transportation. My friends were there, but I didn't want them getting involved with the drama. After all, we were beautiful young ladies, and none of us needed to be fighting in the streets.

Home #7

During my junior year, I started thinking about life after foster care. Being a ward of the state meant no longer going from foster home to foster home. I needed stability. Cathy and Jimmy were very supportive and offered to take care of my son while I pursued a college education. I couldn't imagine leaving my son and going away to college. I was too immature to see the value in the opportunity they were trying to afford me.

I talked with my new caseworker, Gloria, at Boston Children's Services about services available for teen parents. She gave me information about a shelter for teen parents and their children. I completed an application. Being a resident in this program meant I had to adhere to their rules by pursuing my education, having my child in a quality daycare, keeping up with household chores, and, most importantly, following curfew.

There was a house parent who lived on the first floor with her family. She monitored who was coming in and out of apartments and did random checks to make sure our apartments were clean, and ensured we didn't have any guests staying past curfew. There was also an on-site social worker, Linda, who provided resources needed to parent effectively. I started receiving welfare benefits of $224.00 per month and was expected to pay a portion of my income towards rent. I later participated in a voluntary, self-paced life skills curriculum that taught me everything from how to budget to understanding the importance of establishing good credit. Upon completion, I received a stipend of $1,000, which was a great incentive!

I continued going to school and kept my grades up through my senior year. I still spent time with my friends, but also dedicated a lot of time teaching my son. He loved learning new things and was so smart. He also had a great sense of humor and was able to communicate and talked openly with me about things. Our relationship was almost like a big sister caring for her little brother. But he was not my brother; he was my son. I loved him so much I wanted to do everything I could to make sure he didn't have to experience what I did as a child.

I Did It!

I never really took the time to reflect on the day I walked across the stage to receive my high school diploma. Honestly, deep down inside, I didn't expect to do anything less. Although my mother battled through her personal struggles, she planted seeds of expectancy in me at an early age. Her expectations about going to school every day and keeping up my grades led me through a system that was not designed for me to succeed. Even though she never graduated from high school, I believe her desire for her children to have a better chance at life was the reason she pushed us in the direction of prioritizing our education. That was *her* way of showing us love.

Seeing my mother struggle through her addiction was difficult. I wanted to help her but didn't know how. There were times when I saw glimmers of hope, but it was quickly overshadowed by the issues of life. Nevertheless, there was a purpose for MY life. My mother and father were the vessels that brought me into the world. Although the foundation I needed to feel secure throughout my childhood was not present, I was guided by a force greater than any man or woman could ever compete with. That force was with me when I fell in the tub. That force was with me when I hid in my closet. That force was with me when I was hungry. That force was with me through the loss of my mother and birth of my child.

That day, my son, my support system, and closest friends were there, and that was all that mattered. As I sat on the stage, I looked out into the arena with pride, tears rolled down my face because I actually did it. I asked myself the question, "How did I end up on the stage?" Graduating from high school with a baby was not supposed to be. I was supposed to "end up like my mother." Instead, I was graduating with honors and held an office with our student government body at The English High School.

Not only did I walk across the stage, but hundreds of other youths who grew up in the same community walked that day. We walked through the drugs and violence that interrupted our childhood. We walked through having limited resources. We walked through the obstacles that tried to deter us from THE most important thing needed to fight through a system strategically designed to destroy inner-city youth, our education. The English High afforded ME that opportunity. I was LOVED. I was SUPPORTED. I was FREE to be me.

Resolution

When "life" happens, there are things within our control and some out of our control. It is so important to determine what's within your control, then determine the best way to handle it. There are times when we won't know how to handle the curve balls life throws at us; that's when we have to reach out our hand and ask for help. Your help may be through your personal relationship with God or through the people God places in your path, knowingly and unknowingly.

Whether you were born into a "perfect" family or one loaded with dysfunction, I need you to know there is still a purpose for your life. It may take some time to understand your purpose, but whatever you do, DO NOT LOSE HOPE!!! Hope is directly connected to faith. Faith is the very thing that gives us the strength to work through some of the most challenging situations.

My life had purpose. As the little girl at the beginning of this story, I didn't know that, but through a series of events, support from certain individuals, and an earnest desire to want more for my life and my son's life, the pieces of the puzzle started coming together. I could have never done it on my own. If you (and you know who YOU are) played a role in my life, good or bad, with all my heart, I THANK YOU! YOU helped make me better. YOU helped me learn how to navigate through this thing called life. YOU gave me the fuel to keep going.

Closing Remarks

Mrs. Morrison, the mother of my middle school friend, Liz, encouraged me to write my story when I was fourteen years old. When she mentioned it, I heard her, but didn't think too much about it. Later, my eleventh-grade language arts teacher, Ms. Fahey, assigned a writing project. After reading my story, she too, strongly encouraged me to write my story for my son. Until this day, when people hear about my journey, they ask if I've ever considered writing my story. Well, here is a part of it. My plan is to share the next chapter of my life which will include; advocating for teens in Boston, having another child right after graduating high school, being involved in another unhealthy relationship, finding my faith, meeting my husband of now twenty-two years, and finally earning my degree in Human Services & Community Planning. With Lots of Love, Lisa

Special Thanks

I would like to express my gratitude to the following people

Proof-Reader: Kara Fohner

Cover Designer: Jamil Dyair Steele

Photographer: Courtney Jones

Resources

Teen & Tot Program: https://www.bmc.org/pediatrics-teen-and-tot-program

The Teen and Tot Program (TTP) is a comprehensive, innovative, program that works with at-risk and high-risk teens who are dependent on government assistance. The program provides support and education for pregnant and parenting adolescents up to age twenty-one and their children up to age three. The program affords the parent and child to attend their medical appointments together, be seen by the same physician, which allows the doctor to address the needs of both the teen parent and child.

Smart From the Start: https://smartfromthestart.org/

Smart from the Start is a trauma-informed, multi-generational family support and community engagement organization located in the underserved communities of Boston and Washington, DC. It is designed to empower these families with resources and tools to promote the healthy development of young children and families.

Big Brothers Big Sisters of America: https://www.bbbs.org/

Big Brothers Big Sisters seeks to change the lives of children facing adversity forever and for the better. They operate in communities throughout the United States. Mentors work with children in the community, in their schools, on military bases, etc.

Action for Boston and Community Development: https://bostonabcd.org/

ABCD's mission is to empower disadvantaged people by providing them with the tools to overcome poverty, live with dignity, and achieve their full potential.

Cooper Community Center: https://www.cooperctr.org/

The Hattie B. Cooper Community Center has served Greater Roxbury and its surrounding neighborhoods for nearly 100 years, providing under-served children and their families with vital educational programs that facilitate growth and development, while creating opportunities for future successes.